DRAKE'S ISLAND

Once a Fortress now an Adventure Centre

Gun emplacements of the First World War and young people canoeing off the island.

This version of the book is virtually as originally published.
There are now additional pages at the back providing information about the publisher, Arthur L Clamp.

The republishing project is being managed by Arthur's grandson, Steven Gibson. We aim to find all the research that he was involved in publishing, preserving it for the next generation as part of 'The Clamp Collection'.

An Introduction to the Island

Drake's Island, once a fortress and now an adventure centre for young people, is a six acre island situated almost in the middle of Plymouth Sound. It is a focal point for the thousands of visitors who come to Plymouth each year when they view the Sound from Plymouth Hoe taking in Staddon Heights to the east, the thin line of the Breakwater on the seaward side of the Sound and Mount Edgcumbe park on the west side which forms part of the county of Cornwall.

It has been occupied for at least a thousand years and had been owned by the Priors of Plympton Abbey, then by the town of Plymouth and for many years, up until the early 1960's, by the War Department. Its ownership has now reverted to the city of Plymouth. For generations of Plymothians the Island has been a place of mystery. Rumours and gossip added to the mystery. Few private citizens managed to gain access to the Island while it was occupied by troops. One local writer of the last century said *that it was delightful excursion, one which can be made on a summer evening after the usual hours of labour. The island is a spot interesting for the associations it so forcibly brings to the mind of the days when men could scarce think as they list and when to speak their thoughts consigned them to prison.*

Fortunately for local people and visitors every step is now being taken to encourage them to go to Drake's Island and see for themselves the many interesting military features still in position, the young people engaged in adventure course work and, perhaps for the first time, view Plymouth from a point not previously seen. The Island's position gives a panoramic view of Plymouth's shoreline backed by fine houses and Smeaton's tower on the Hoe. An excellent view of the Sound will be obtained from the top of the island, a grandstand position during the summer months when the area will normally be dotted with small craft of many descriptions. The nearest part of Plymouth to the Island is Stonehouse and the Millbay docks area from which the Roscoff ferry links the city with France.

The Island is formed of hard volcanic rock, is a little over six acres in area and reaches a height of 96 feet. It was originally part of a rocky ledge which protrudes into the Sound from Mount Edgcumbe parallel to the limestone rock face of the present Plymouth foreshore. Most of this has been worn away by tides and river water flowing into the sea. The remaining ledge, known as the *Bridge*, can be seen at very low water and has been used to advantage by the military authorities in helping to defend the large naval dockyard in Devonport. There is a deep water channel running between the Island and the nearest foreshore of the city. To the west of the Island stands Little Drake's Island which is quite accessible except at high tide.

The strategic role which this small Island has played in the defence of the area came about because of its prime position overlooking the main water channel through which all large ships must pass in order to reach Devonport Dockyard. Prior to the yard's development in the 1690's the naval port facilities were located in the much older Sutton harbour and Cattedown areas well to the east of the island, overlooked by the Royal Citadel built on the Hoe during the 1660's. The Island fortifications were part of a much larger scheme for defending the area. There were batteries covering the sea approaches from Mount Edgcumbe, the channel from Western and Eastern King's Points (the nearest foreshore to the island) and from the Citadel for the western part of the Sound. Any attack by invaders upon the vast dockyard complex would have to be preceded by one on Drake's Island destroying its fire power before being able to get any closer. The more direct entrance between the Island and Mount Edgcumbe could only be made by very small craft as the rocky ledge had been made more difficult to cross by laying down large rocks and obstacles, one line of which is now known as the *Dragon's teeth*. It can be appreciated why the casemates were positioned where they are on the Island as these would be the first of the defending batteries to engage an enemy attack from the sea.

This 1939 deep water pier is the Island's landing place.

Since 1963 the Island has taken on a new lease of life as an adventure centre for young people of all nations and now comes under the management of the Mayflower Trust. Its position, facilities and the opportunities for young people to accept its challenges for personal development and achievement promise Drake's Island a future befitting the role it has played for the past 500 years. It is with these thoughts in mind that thanks and appreciation are recorded here to many people who have helped in the preparation of this publication. Special thanks are due to Mr. Stanley Goodman for supplying much of the detailed information about the island's armaments, to Ian Hogg, the staff of the City library, administrative office in the Mayflower Centre to and to those actually manning the Island.

The Early Years on St. Nicholas Island, 1135-1599

The island first appears in records around the year 1135 when an entry in Plymouth's archives states that Saint Michael's island, its original name, was transferred to the Priors of Plympton together with its "conies" by the Norman family of Valletorts who were then overlords of the town.

This is almost certainly not the only event to have taken place here during those early years especially in view of the island's position in the Sound. There may well have been some form of warning beacon working here during bad weather conditions and the reference to its rabbits, bred away from predators on the mainland, does give some indication of an earlier and profitable use as a source of winter meat for the townspeople.

There was a chapel here, dedicated to St. Michael, standing on the highest point of the island, which was probably the first building to be erected on it. Its name was later changed to St. Nicholas, patron saint of sailors, a common dedication around the coastline. This name remained until about 1590 when it was changed to the present name in honour of one of Plymouth's most illustrious sons, Sir Francis Drake.

In the reign of Richard II (1377-1399) the island is recorded as having had some kind of bonded warehouse where goods were landed and held until certain dues had been paid unless they were placed on sale. This reference is not very clear but it could have been that the Island was used as a store for goods which were not immediately required by Plymouth. A record of this period refers to *merchants and seamen, native and foreign, coming to and touching a place called Conners on St. Nicholas island.*

The first Fortifications, 1550

A new and much more important role for the island commenced around the year 1550 when the old chapel was demolished and the first of many schemes of fortification was started by a bulwark being constructed of stones and turf around its higher contours. There was then general alarm along the coast as a result of the French Wars and the Privy Council had requested Plymouth to take steps to make this important naval base more secure against attack from the sea. An indenture dated 1549 was made between King Edward VI and the Mayor for the upkeep of a fort on the island. William Hawkins was paid £100 for the fortifications along the Hoe and on the island together with *five fodders of lead* for covering the buildings at an extra charge.

The island was garrisoned for in 1551 it is recorded that the Privy Council paid £79 1s.8d. to Plymouth for *the wages of 4 gunners, one at 8d. by the day, and others at 6d. by the day, serving in the fort of St. Nicholas Island for two whole years.* Part of the cost was met from customs dues although over the next few years various arguments took place over who was responsible for them. The Island then belonged to Plymouth yet it was the government which requested its defence.

In 1583 it was petitioned that Sir Francis Drake be made the Island's governor and it is from about this date that the Island changed its name. In the same decade Plymouth relinquished its ownership of the island to the state which took in *the fortification, continuance, maintenance, artillery, furniture and munitions to be used in or upon the defence of St. Nicholas Island for the defence of the same.*

The old town of Plymouth and the defences around the Sound.

The Island's Fortifications and its use as a Prison, 1600-1699

It had become increasingly clear to the authorities that Drake's Island, to use its new name, would play a key role in the defence of Plymouth and as such must receive more attention and money than was first planned around 1550.

There had been a series of enquiries into how this should be done, various important people had come from London to inspect schemes and different recommendations had been made from time to time. Drake had pressed for an enquiry in 1591 to examine all the defences of Plymouth and in 1592 Robert Adams, a military engineer, stressed that the Island must be included in any overall plan for this area.

The Island was further strengthened under the direction of Adams, the work of which was reported by a Spanish spy to include between forty and fifty guns and the Island garrison of about 100 men.

One famous military engineer, Frederico Genibelli, who had helped in the preparations to resist the Armada, later laid down plans for increasing the Island's defences. In 1602 he wrote to Sir Robert Cecil, *having provided materials and workmen, begun to work on the houses in the island for the lodging of soldiers and also on the wall of the parapet about the island.* He went on to complain about the weather hindering his progress.

The governorship of the Hoe fort and island passed to Sir Ferdinando Gorges and in 1599 he was instructed to erect barricades on the rocks and construct barracks to house the garrison which had been increased to 300 men. This was to meet the threat of a Spanish retaliatory attack after the crushing defeat in 1588 (the defeat of the Armada).

It appears that during the opening years of this century the Island defences were neglected and that when war broke out in 1627 100 men were lodged on the Island in readiness for fighting in the Channel Islands at a charge of £16 per week. The fighting did not take place and they were dismissed from the service. Sir Ferdinando Gorges retired as governor in 1627 having been in that post for about thirty years.

The Civil War and the Island State Prison, 1642-1684
This tragic war broke out in 1642 and Plymouth declared for Parliament. It successively withstood a siege by the Royalist troops and the island played an important role during those difficult days. When Sir Jacob Astley quitted the governorship of the fort and Island in 1642 the Mayor and corporation took charge appointing Sir Alexander Carew in his place. Unfortunately for Plymouth he was suspected of treason — refusing to come ashore from the Island even to collect his pay. Eventually he was arrested and beheaded on Tower Hill, London, on 23rd December, 1644. Had he allowed the royalist troops to land on the Island Plymouth could hardly have withstood the Royalist siege.

Henry Hatsell, a trusted Parliamentarian soldier was put in command of Drake's Island during the remainder of the siege and under his direction it was strengthened and heavily manned. The garrison cost £295 8s. 0d. per month to maintain, a large sum for the town to bear.

The Royalists' cause failed, Cromwell was appointed to head the new government and the siege of Plymouth was raised. New establishments were drawn up for the defence of Plymouth which included for Drake's Island *a governor, a preacher, a gunsmith, a surgeon, a storekeeper, a master gunner, two gunners, six gunners' mates, twelve mattresses, two bootmen, together with two companies of foot soldiers of 100 each and their officers, a captain, a lieutenant and an ensign for each company.* The Island was one of the main keys to the defence of the town; it would not be neglected again.

The restoration of the monarchy took place in 1660 when King Charles II was crowned. The outlook for Plymouth was not good and many of its citizens were deprived of their positions and the town itself was subjected to the watchful eye of the new order. The citadel on the Hoe was started in the 1660's by order of the King with the double purpose of increasing the protection of the port and maintaining a close watch over the once rebellious citizens.

Drake's Island was now used as a state prison in which were confined some important parliamentarian figures. It was a sad era for the Island and lasted about twenty five years, as reports of the conditions under which some of the prisoners were

The Island's entrance dating from Tudor times.

kept were deplorable. The most prominent person to be sent to the island was Major-General John Lambert who had hoped to succeed Cromwell as Lord Protector. He was transferred from a prison on Guernsey to Plymouth in 1670 and was then confined to the Island until he died in 1684. He had visitors, one of whom wrote that *he had lost his memory and sense* and another, Yonge, that *Lambert, that old rebel, died this winter on Plymouth Island where he had been prisoner 15 years and more.*

Another notable prisoner, the first to go to the Island, was Colonel Robert Lilburn who took an active part in the Civil War and was one of the judges who condemned Charles I to death. Upon his trial in 1660 he was sentenced to death but this was later commuted to life imprisonment. In 1661 a warrant directed that he should be sent *as a condemned traitor close prisoner to Plymouth castle or St. Nicholas Island, whichever the governors of Plymouth should think safe.*

Other prisoners were confined to the island for political reasons; among them was James Harrington, a republican and author of "Commonwealth of Oceana", published in 1656. He was later allowed to leave the Island and live in Plymouth for health reasons. It was only to be expected that some of the local people involved in the siege would also be confined to the island. Some who suffered this fate were George Hughes, the Presbyterian vicar of Plymouth's main church, St. Andrews, his assistant, Thomas Martyn and Abraham Cheare a Baptist minister from the town, who died on the Island after three year's confinement.

Charles II visited Plymouth on a number of occasions to inspect the work on the Citadel and during one visit he was taken to the island to see Lambert. Samuel Pepys also recorded in his diary that while in Plymouth he was taken over to see the noted Parliamentarian prisoner. During the Civil War one report spoke of Parliamentarian prisoners being kept there who had been captured during campaigns in Ireland. Unfortunately there are very few details about these men other than that they had been taken during the struggles. Nothing more is heard of the Island being used as a prison after the death of its last prisoner, Abraham Cheare, in 1668.

A few years later the role of the Island as an important feature in the defence of the town increased considerably when the decision was taken to move the dockyard facilities serving the navy from the Cattewater to the banks of the river Tamar in what is now Devonport. This move was made in 1691, and gave added point to the need to strengthen the defences on the Island. Its position at, and control of the mouth of the Tamar was of paramount importance to the security of the growing dock complex and the volume of ship building taking place. All vessels entering or leaving the dock had to pass within a very short distance of the Island while following the deep water channel running between it and Plymouth's foreshore at Stonehouse. It was this move which determined the role which the Island was to play during the next 250 years.

It is not known how the island was actually defended during its early years of fortification apart from the references to the number of guns deployed on it and the garrison needed to man and operate them. It

The musketry wall on the west side of the island.

is most likely that the top and higher land of the Island was the position from which most of the guns would have been fired had there been any attack upon Plymouth. The entrance gate and small courtyard is generally thought to have been constructed during one of the many schemes intended to make the Island impregnable to soldiers trying to capture it from invading ships. The limestone wall to the west of the barrack block is also thought to date from this time. It was constructed with openings through which muskets could be aimed at attackers.

A similarly styled building but perhaps of an earlier period, is the plain looking single windowed structure overlooking the rocks on the north side of the island. It is believed to be an *oubliette* — a cell or dungeon in which prisoners were lowered and left to die. Access is through an opening in the roof and there is just a single room below. Very few of these are known to exist in England.

The Military Occupation, 1700-1899

The opening years of the eighteenth century saw new proposals for bringing up to date and strengthening the defences of Drake's Island which were made more necessary through the development of the naval dockyard on the banks of the Hamoaze. In 1701 a report recommended that two batteries on the Island, one of nineteen guns and the other of fourteen, be set up as soon as possible. A few years later in 1717 a Colonel Lilley reported on all the defences of Plymouth stating that those on the Island were ruinous and not capable of holding off attacks for any length of time. An outlay of £7,000 would be required to adequately defend it.

It appears that by this date the various improvements made during the previous century were very much neglected. Some remains from these early fortifications are still on the Island. The entrance gate and small courtyard, with its musket ledge, the musket wall on the west of the island and probably the sentry walk which overlooks the slipway to the left of the pier are some of them. There has been so much construction work undertaken at later periods that it is very fortunate that anything at all is left from the seventeenth century.

The responsibility for manning the guns and maintaining the service equipment fell to a corps of gunners of a semi-military nature under the control of the Board of Ordnance. This dated back to 1540 and was reasonably adequate during peace time. However, in times of war or expectations of attack, marching companies were brought in to aid them from the Royal Regiment of Artillery. This Regiment formed in 1716 but it was not until 1771 that the regiment took over the manning of coastal defences, a role which it had undertaken until recent years. In 1771 eight Royal Artillery Invalid (or Pensioner) companies were formed from the older personnel of the regiment and these, together with a corps of gunners, manned coastal defences around the country.

During the American War of Independence there was a threat of invasion in 1779 from France and Spain and it was expected that a landing would be made in Cawsand Bay, just a few miles along the Cornish coast. The strength of the local garrison would not have thrown off the attack. There were only ninety-six gunners to man guns in the Citadel and on Drake's Island which then possessed twenty-one 32 pounders and two 18 pounders. The French fleet did actually set sail and was sighted off Plymouth but fortunately an easterly gale was blowing which took the ships down channel to Brest. Further measures to strengthen the defences of the Island were listed in a report of 1763 as: On the works of Saint Nicholas Island are mounted twenty-three 32 pounders, six 18 pounders and two brass 13 inch mortars. There are two small magazines lately constructed here which will contain all the stores and shot. Master gunners from the Artillery Regiment manned the actual guns assisted by Invalid gunners who undertook the preservation and maintenance of each battery.

War with Revolutionary France broke out in 1793 and the defences of Plymouth were consequently improved and more men were drafted in bringing the strength of the Plymouth militia to two marching companies of the Royal Artillery supported by local volunteer corps. Fortunately again for Plymouth the troubles in France had no material effect on the area although the years were not without their fair share of rumours and counter rumours. The complement of guns and men on the island was increased but with the coming of peace in 1802 there were considerable reductions made in troops on coastal defence stations.

The former Commanding Officer's house constructed in the 183

From 1816 until 1846 there was one Royal Artillery company stationed in the Plymouth area part of whose work was the manning of the Island. It is likely that very little was done on Drake's Island during these years and much of the then existing fortifications were left to deteriorate. The extensive works constructed during the latter half of the last century and the reports made about existing facilities made this quite plain. The Invalid companies were disbanded in 1819 although some personnel were retained to assist the master gunners. In 1824 there were two of these at Plymouth, one at the Citadel and the other, George Mahon, on the Island. There were then five assistant invalids all stationed in the Citadel. The Barrack Return of 1822 gives the strength of the Island detachment as two officers and seventy-two men. A company of the 32nd Foot (Duke of Cornwall's Light Infantry) was stationed on the Island in 1825 for which there was building accommodation for three officers and ninety-six men. A later return in 1847 gives additional information about the accommodation stating that there were twenty rooms for sleeping, an ablution room and cookhouse. Eight privates slept per room while the sergeants had one room each. Between the dates of these two returns was built the existing barrack block in the years 1830-35. The reference to the ablutions is to the building behind the barracks. These are the buildings now used for accommodating young people on the adventure courses. The barrack

A view of the granite casemates built in the 1860's.

block is the largest of the three main buildings beyond the entrance gate, the rear one being the ablution block. The nearest building to the entrance to the island was also built in the 1830's and was the Commanding Officer's house. There was yet another and more detailed report on the Island's accommodation in 1859. This gave details of the living quarters for 130 men and was very critical of the various provisions for living and sleeping here and made many suggestions for improving them. The room referred then to as the Island's hospital, consisted of one ward which was being used as a reading room and school room. The kitchen was inadequate and the actual living space for each man was far too small.

This period was to be a major turning point not only for Drake's Island but for the whole system of coastal defence, the weapons used, their increased fire power and the procedures to be followed in case of attack. While a coast gunner of 1700 would have recognised his counterpart in 1815 and the guns then still being used this resemblance would not have been the case between 1815 and some fifty to seventy-five years later.

A close view of the iron shield and outer face of the casemates.

Enormous advances were taking place in the manufacture of armaments and new methods of handling had to be developed. These were brought about by the Industrial Revolution and the advance in scientific knowledge. Drake's Island and its fortifications were to change radically because of these factors and the new and alarming changes in warship construction and fire power first developed by the French. Their new steam-driven ironclads presented serious challenges for coastal defence systems and changes in methods of attacks had to be matched by changes in defence.

The need to strengthen the defences had been appreciated in 1846 for in Plymouth in that year the existing single company of Royal Artillery was increased to three or more and a number of militia artillery companies were newly formed from the county infantry regiments. This took place in 1853. In 1859 the Royal Artillery was completely re-organised and special provision was made for coastal defence duties. The Invalid Detachment, (formed in 1819) was disbanded and the care and maintenance duties became the responsibility of a new body, the Coast Brigade. There were still master gunners in this new body but these were serving Royal Artillery

Young visitors to the island astride the 25 ton guns.

personnel of Warrant Officer rank. The moves that brought about the 1859 reorganisation and the deployment of more personnel on coastal defence duties also resulted in a detailed examination of the actual defences themselves in 1860 from which many of the present military features on the island, including the casemates, arose. At the time of this report there was a battery of guns made up of eight 8 inch, five 56 pounders, six 30 pounders and three 8 inch howitzers on the island, quite inadequate to cope with any attack by the new class of French warships with their heavy fire power.

In the 1860's work was started on building the formidable casemates to hold very large guns for the defence of the main water channel running to the east of the island and north between the mainland and the Island's foreshore through which all warships had to pass before entering the dockyard. A progress report on the schemes of construction in 1867 stated *at*

Drake's Island, a casemated battery for twenty-one 12 ton guns, at a level of 38 ft. 6 ins. above high water, has been constructed of granite prepared for the reception of iron shields. It is further intended to make provision for mounting five 23 ton guns on a higher level, en barbette, with earthern traverses between each gun. These are the guns unearthed in 1978 on the top of the island.

A further report elaborated on the scheme as *there is a large magazine in the rear entirely protected from fire, communicating by subterranean galleries with the expense magazines immediately in rear of the passage behind the casemates.* It went on to say *the upper battery was designed for a barbette to mount five of the heaviest rifled guns. The foundations are on rock and the work is well and skillfully designed.* In 1862 the estimate for this was £35,000, the estimate for the iron shields £27,000 which together with other supporting work brought the total sum to approximately £63,500.

The line drawing of the casemate battery scheme on this page gives a good indication of the Island's major military feature. Much of it will not be seen by the visitor as many of the side passages and rooms at the rear of the casemates still await a thorough investigation into their original use. Later modifications have made it difficult to identify the function of many of the smaller rooms and safety factors prevent all of them being open to the public. The main features of the scheme have been named in the drawing.

In 1870 a Defence Committee was set up to deal with the whole matter of coastal defence throughout the country which reported in 1886 on the armament of the Island as: Lower battery, west face, six 80 pounders; south face, two 64/32 pounders. Main battery, three 11 inch and two 12 inch guns. Casemated battery, south-east face, eleven 9 inch guns; east face, two 9 inch guns. Lower battery, east face, two 8 inch howitzers; open emplacement, one 18 pounder. The Island was now well and truly fortified and ready should an attack be made by the new class of French warships. No such attack came and, apart from practice shots, the guns were never used.

A similar reorganisation of the Royal Artillery took place at the same time and various batteries from the 8th Brigade, which was stationed in Plymouth, saw service on the Island during these hazardous years. For instance in December, 1877, the detachment came from no. 3 battery made up of forty-four men with one officer. It seems likely that during the last quarter of the century the number of men stationed on the Island was in the region of forty to fifty. The fears of an attack had passed and the Island's complement of troops was accordingly reduced. A later reorganisation in 1899 brought together garrison batteries and the coast brigades to form (within the Royal Artillery) the Royal Garrison Artillery. The closing years of the nineteenth century brought to an end one of the most active periods of the military use of this small strategic Island in Plymouth Sound. Had the expected attack taken place the noise of the giant guns would have reverberated from shore to shore and the outcome of the attack might well have been determined by the effectiveness of these fortifications. It is difficult, if not impossible, to conjure up the atmosphere of this period, the great amount of activity taking place not only on the Island but all around Plymouth where today many forts still stand as reminders of those far-off times. Out of all the forts encircling Plymouth, those remaining on the Island with their underground shell and cartridge stores linked to access tunnels are the most vivid reminders of those days.

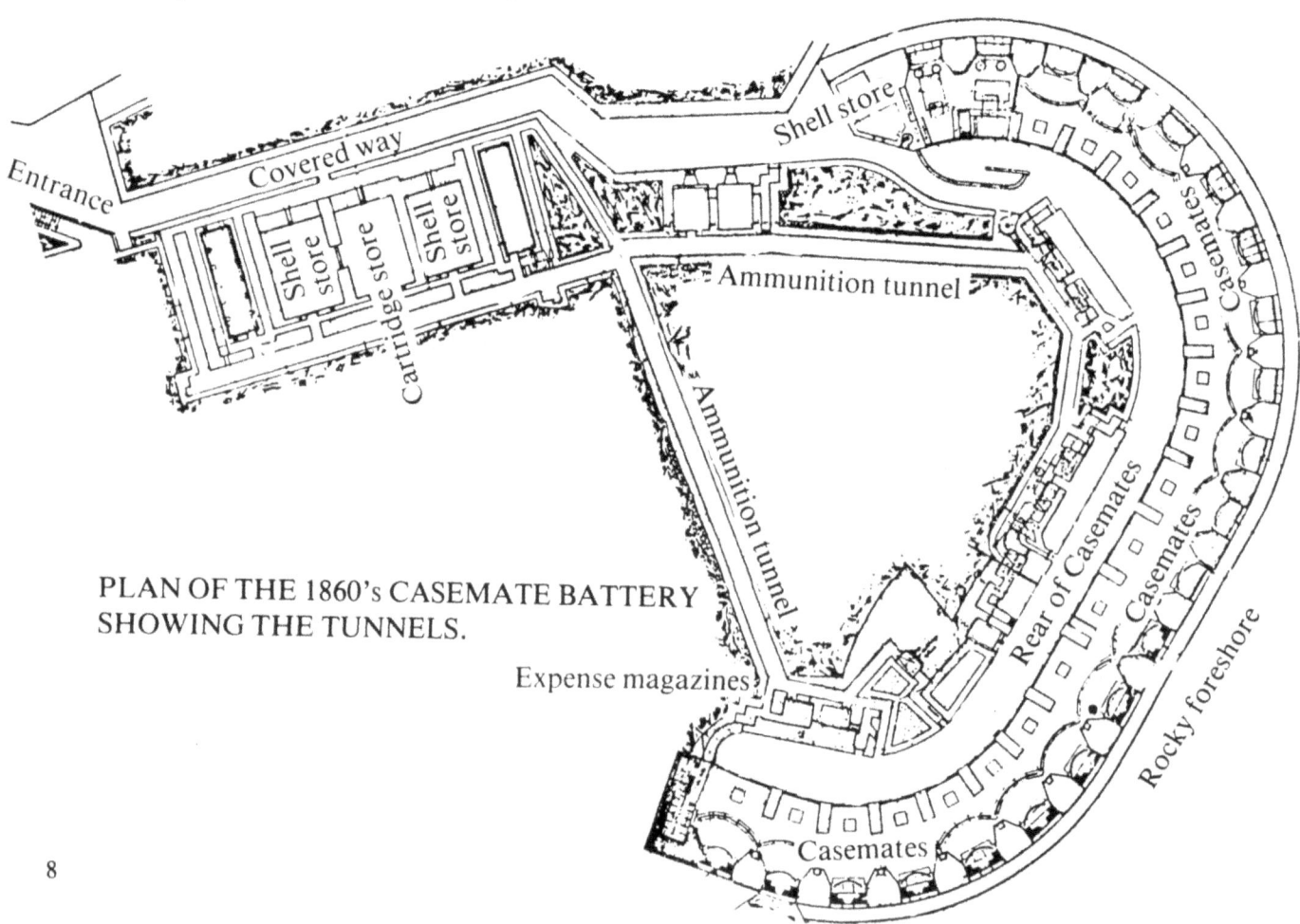

PLAN OF THE 1860's CASEMATE BATTERY SHOWING THE TUNNELS.

The Role of the Island, 1900-1956

This period in the history of Drake's Island was predominantly influenced by the two World Wars which, for the whole of the Plymouth area, brought drastic changes in military personnel stationed in the various camps, including the manning of the Island, and the direct involvement of the city during 1939-45 through the extensive devastation of the blitz. In spite of these major occurrences the Island emerged unscathed and the closing years of its military use passed without any significant events taking place unless the blowing up of many of the Island's fortifications by the Army prior to their evacuation could be classed as such.

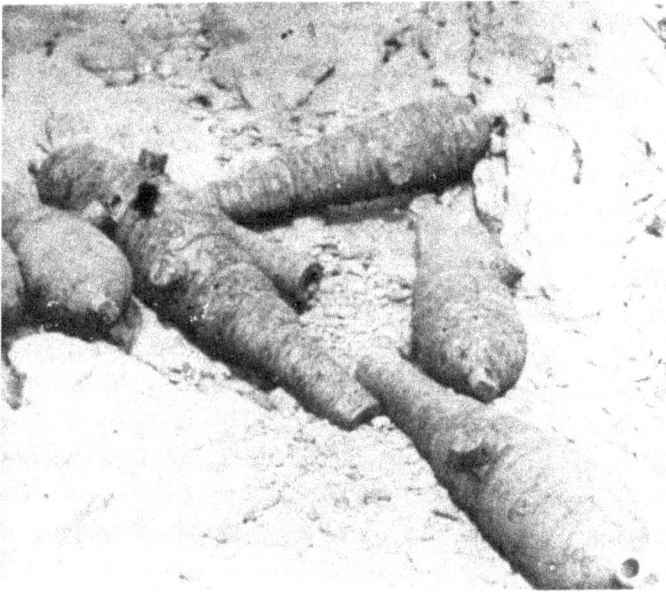

Seven discarded old rifled muzzle loading guns left on the island's shore from about 1905 to 1940.

During the years before the outbreak of war in 1914 the armament on the island was three 12 pounder quick-firing guns in the lower battery, three 6 inch breech-loading guns in the main battery and three 12 pounder quick-firing guns in the casemates. There were three officers and sixty-nine non-commissioned men on duty. In 1914 the returns showed then that four officers, eleven sergeants, two trumpeters and 134 rank and file were stationed on the island from no. 45 company which garrisoned it until 1918 when it was entrusted to a new body, no. 3 Fire Command. At the close of the war in 1918 the troops numbered twenty officers, five warrant officers, four sergeants, two trumpeters and 178 rank and file.

The concrete gun emplacements along the top of the Island date from at least 1914 and make up the Island's main fortifications constructed this century. These were serviced from underground shell stores linked by tunnels which are now cleared. Searchlights were also operational from this period, powered by engines installed in the first of the casemates and sited in front of them. Seven old 9 inch rifled-muzzled loading guns were discarded from their positions around this time and were left close to the pier beach (see photographs) until they were cut up in 1940 for scrap.

The inter-war years saw considerable changes in the organisation of troops responsible for manning the Island whose establishment in 1932 consisted of one captain, one district officer, two master gunners, one sergeant, one bombardier, three tradesmen, four gunners and five civilian district gunners. This Fire Command unit covered the defence of the nearby mainland as well.

In 1939 there were two 6 inch and five 12 pounder guns on the Island but within a month or two of hostilities some of these were removed and others took their place. A 40 m.m. A.A. gun was installed, the present pier constructed, the slipway strengthened, an ammunition hoist (replaced by the present new one) built and a tall gunnery control erected on top of the island which was demolished by the army in the 1950's. There were also concrete bunkers built, gun sites strengthened and a minefield control post operational from the island which would have detonated mines placed over much of the Sound, had an invasion taken place. By April, 1941, there were 490 troops stationed on this key Island. The number remained around this figure for most of the war. In spite of the German raids on Plymouth and its dockyard the island only suffered slightly from thirty-one incendiaries and several high explosive bombs falling on and around it. One person was injured and the canteen roof was damaged. The 40 m.m. gun engaged an enemy aircraft on 13th June, 1944.

The end of the war heralded for Drake's Island its last years as a military fortress during which its use and value to the overall defence plans of the country diminished to such an extent that by the 1950's it was deemed unnecessary to man it any longer. The scale and change in warfare through harnessing the atom finally brought to an end hundreds of years of military occupation and gave opportunities for this small Island to be put to other uses. In 1956 the Minister of Defence announced that the Coast Artillery was to be disbanded at which time the Island had six 12 pounder guns still operational and manned by twelve officers, eleven W.O.'s and N.C.O.'s and 114 rank and file. In December, 1956, Ministry of Supply contractors removed all the armaments and fittings and demolished much of the gun positions and other military features built during the last war.

One of the island's First World War searchlights.

The three upper illustrations on this page were taken by a soldier while on duty here in 1914 and are part of an extensive collection showing different aspects of life on the island from the hand-operated fire engine, the start of the annual *Battleaxe* parade and an inspection of the casemates. The lower two show a shell hoist, still in position, and a six inch breech-loading gun dating at least from the First World War in position on the island.

Shipwrecks around the Island

The coastline of Devon and Cornwall is strewn with the remains of hundreds of shipwrecks, both large and small, dating back many years. The sea lanes used by shipping to enter the various ports were especially dangerous for the sailing ships which were completely dependent upon a good steady and reliable wind to make port. However, the very close presence of the coastline and the change in temperature from the land to the sea gives rise to variable and local wind conditions which often resulted in a ship going aground.

Plymouth Sound and the surrounding coastline was no exception to the pattern of shipwrecks along the south-western shores. The sea approaches to Plymouth were especially dangerous to shipping because of the Eddystone reef a few miles out to sea. One of the determining factors in the building of the Plymouth breakwater in the last century was the need for additional protection to shipping sheltering in the Sound and to reduce to a minimum the effect of a strong south-west wind blowing up the channel and preventing sailing ships from leaving the Sound. Ships were often storm bound in the Cattewater waiting for a change in the wind direction before being able to tack across the Sound and out into the Channel.

Although Drake's Island is quite small it stands near to the main tidal flow of the large Tamar river and its shore faces the centre of the Sound and, as a consequence, has had its due proportion of wrecks, even large men-of-war such as the seventy-gun *H.M.S. Conqueror* which went ashore in 1760.

One of the earliest wrecks on the island was the *Lavinia*, a prize vessel captured from the French which dragged her anchors during a gale until she hit the rocks. There must have been many before this date but no records tell of the disasters or of the seamen who often lost their lives as well. No doubt this was one of the main reasons why a beacon had originally been placed on the island and the later chapel which had also acted as a beacon during bad weather.

In 1637 the East India ship, *Paulsgrove* was lost on Drake's Island through the insistence of her captain or leaving the Sound during a storm. Waves prevented her from getting out into the open sea and she parted her cable before being washed ashore.

Reference has already been made about the 1760 disaster of *H.M.S. Conqueror*. She was the largest ship to go aground on the Island and had only been in service for two years. The records tell that the pilot was to blame. He was imprisoned for eighteen months.

From time to time great storms have occurred causing a very large amount of damage to the old sailing ships and wrecking many around the Sound. Great winter storms have been recorded for 1637, 1799, 1804, 1810 and 1824. Although the numerous wrecks counted after the storms were not definitely identified according to where they took place, many of them must have occurred on the Island as this small length of rocky shore was the first piece of land encountered when coming into the Sound.

A later wreck took place in 1868, this time a small vessel, the Brixham sloop *Uncle Jack* with the loss of the five-member crew. Finally in 1914 the *Ernia*, a ninety-one ton schooner from Bremen, was forced to run for shelter during a gale. She dragged her anchor and later ran ashore on the Island where she broke up. All six crew were saved by the Plymouth lifeboat.

The "Bridge" between the Island and Mount Edgcumbe.

Mr. Day's Diving machine, 1798

Another wreck of quite a different kind occurred at a point between the Island and the mainland in 1798. A certain Mr. Day from Suffolk had invented what was described as a diving machine in which he claimed that a man could live for a time under water.

This attracted great attention, especially locally, when his second experiment of going down twenty-eight fathoms took place offshore opposite the island. He had built a small vessel with a false bottom which held stones and was attached by means of movable pins worked within. On the 20th June, 1798, Mr. Day provided himself with a hammock, watch, wax taper, bottle of water and some biscuits before raising the vessel's hatch and climbing in. He was confident that he would reach the seabed and remain there for twelve hours before releasing the pins and allowing the vessel to rise to the surface. He would also release three small buoys to indicate that all was well.

After a false start his vessel slowly sank below the water and the crowds hopefully watched for the first buoy to break surface. Unfortunately nothing happened apart from bubbles rising a moment after the vessel had gone down. Following the twelve hours, attempts were made to locate the vessel but without success. The experiment failed and in spite of a wide search no trace of it was found.

Drake's Island Adventure Centre

This title for the Island very fittingly describes its role as one of the country's foremost centres for providing sea and land based courses of adventure for young people. Although there was some uncertainty around 1960 as to what kind of use the island could be put to the initial response to the then immediate problem of clearing up the island and making its buildings once more habitable soon gave way to various ideas on making a bold start towards putting it on the national map as an adventure centre. A better setting could not have been found. The West Country is the main holiday area for the whole of the United Kingdom and Plymouth takes it annual share in providing visitors with relaxing and enjoyable opportunities for recreation on land and sea. The new link with France and Spain, through the channel ferries from Plymouth, has given more and much wider scope for visitors to reach this part of the country.

Drake's Island in its setting and almost in the middle of the south-west peninsula, has given an additional opportunity to the wide range of courses, holidays and places to visit in the county and it can now claim that its new role is unique in this most popular of holiday areas.

Towards the end of the 1950's army contractors set about blowing up the military features on the island and had filled in gun positions and last war posts. Fortunately the earlier fortifications were not damaged although they had been modified for wartime use and at least two concrete posts and some minor features were left from this last military interesting as the much earlier remains but time will clothe them with plants and mature the stonework to blend a little with the granite and limestone already there.

The first years of the 1960's were not good ones for the Island. There was a scene of desolation over much of its surface, the building had fallen into decay and the roofs were letting in the elements. The War Department finally released the island in 1963 and, through the National Trust, it was leased to Plymouth as a Youth Training Base. In the same year the first warden, Mr. S. Bennet, was appointed. He undertook a large amount of work until leaving in 1966. The first years were extremely difficult ones as tons of debris had to be moved and repair work put in hand to the various buildings and the pier and slipway.
At the same time, the idea of its new use had to be promoted and young people encouraged to use it. Even the fairly straight forward matter of obtaining fresh running water presented problems which were resolved in 1964 by laying a pipe from the mainland. Financial support was given by the City to the new project and grants were made by various bodies towards the Island's running costs. In 1964 the Island was officially opened for the first time to the public for a limited period which was later extended.

In 1974 the island was redesignated as *Drake's Island Adventure Centre* and its administration was undertaken by the Mayflower Centre Trust which is also responsible for the Mayflower Sports Centre in Plymouth. The administration for the island is now undertaken from Central Park, Plymouth, and additional and new schemes of work on the Island and courses have been undertaken. The opportunities for the development of the island as an adventure centre are now greater and support from young people for its courses has increased very considerably over the past few years.

One of the many challenges confronting young people on the Island's courses is that of scaling this steep wall.

The rocks and pools at low tide provide an abundant source of marine life for examination.

The centre is now open all the year round and offers a wide range of adventure based courses and holidays for young people of all nationalities. Young boys and girls over eight years of age can attend courses on a residential or, for local youngsters, a non-residential basis for periods of one, two or three weeks' duration.

Groups

The residential groups are made up of boys and girls twelve years or over and come from a variety of backgrounds. School groups are the most popular as the Island's course work complements that done in school. Other groups come from industry or commerce, scout troups, foreign students groups and groups requiring particular schedules of training. A number of individuals also spend part of their holiday here who are sponsored by employers or organisations engaged in supporting young people. Non-residential courses can be taken by boys and girls eight years or over and come mainly from the Plymouth area.

Residential groups and individuals come to Drake's Island from many parts of England and the British Isles. Various groups from overseas have also undertaken courses here, normally coming to Plymouth via the Channel ferry. The local boys and girls come over the island on the daily boat which leaves from Mayflower Steps.

During the more popular months of July and August a wide range of holidays and activities are available to cater for the needs and progressive standards in the adventure training programmes.

Visitors to the island are sometimes surprised and pleased to see handicapped children participate in the courses which are organised in consultation with the sponsoring organisation. The adventure training facilities are open to all young people.

Accommodation

There is dormitory accommodation for ninety-six students plus supporting staff in rooms holding between six and fourteen beds. Showers, drying rooms, quiet and recreational areas and lecture rooms are available for use by young people on the various courses. Catering facilities are of a high standard and ably cope with the day to day needs of groups living on the island.

Training courses

All the programmes are arranged in consultation with the appropriate sponsoring body and cover sailing, canoeing, rock climbing, orienteering, caving, marine biology and expeditions. They run continuously throughout the day while most evenings are devoted to sport, films, safety drills and activities linked to the theme of the course.

The very fine opportunities for sailing in the Sound are not missed and boats will often be seen visiting nearby Jennycliff, Cawsand and going up the Tamar to Saltash. The range of Island boats include Wayfarers, other sailing dinghies and cruising yachts. Safety launches are always on duty during the training periods. The canoeing is always under the watchful eye of an experienced instructor. The rock climbing challenges take place on the south facing buttress of the island, on the climbing wall, and on Dartmoor; again under very careful guidance by experienced personnel with all the necessary safety equipment in use. These activities start from the Island pier and introductory sessions take place close by where groups of boats or canoes will be seen by the Island's visitors.

The need for training in map and compass reading is catered for by facilities here and at Mount Edgcumbe County Park on the Cornwall side of

A group of young people about to climb one of the Island's cliffs.

Plymouth Sound. Special orienteering routes and courses are prepared which give experience in this sport for groups of different ages. Marine biology and its study may not attract everyone but this fascinating and often overlooked aspect of coastal life stimulates the minds of many youngsters here once having spent a few days on the island. The rocky foreshore provides many opportunities for finding out about the less apparent forms of sea life and specimens for study can be collected from the shoreline or from boats. All courses require some form of safety or special clothing which is provided as part of the programme.

Staff

An experienced team of instructors is responsible for the various training programmes under the direction of a Chief Instructor. The students are grouped into training classes of twelve which gives an average staff to student ratio of one to five although this will vary according to the nature of the activity. The Island centre has supporting maintenance and catering staff and boatmen for bringing students and visitors to Drake's Island. Additional information about the centre can be obtained from the Mayflower Sports Centre, Central Park, Plymouth.

The Island's future

The past fifteen years have seen great changes on the Island, more people have been here, either on courses or as day visitors, during this period than probably for any other since it was first occupied hundreds of years ago. Drake's Island has been brought to the notice of many people working in youth activities and the tourist industry in the West Country and what was once an island banned to the public is now fast becoming a well known place for people holidaying in Devon and Cornwall.

There is still a great amount of work to do both to uncover more of its fascinating past and increase the facilities for its new role as an adventure centre. As recently as 1978 we uncovered the very large guns which were part of the upper battery. Who knows what may still be buried under the island and whether

there will be any truth in suggestions that dungeons are here?

The prospect for the Island's development as a centre for youth activities is almost boundless with the opportunities for sea-based courses in Plymouth Sound and an increasing emphasis being placed by schools and organisations on encouraging young people to use their initiative and resource. A lot of ground work has already been done in building up the Centre to extend its facilities and open its doors to more young people.

Exploring the Island

a. The Landing Pier
This is the obvious place to start a tour of Drake's Island The pier was constructed in 1939 in preparation for handling considerable supplies and ammunition for the duration of the 1939-45 war which, fortunately, were not required. Although Plymouth itself suffered many devastating air raids the Island only received minor damage in spite of its guns assisting in defending the city. A slipway and crane were also built at the same time. One of the Island's two small sandy beaches is by the pier which visitors take advantage of when waiting for the return boat. It is from here that the Island's canoeing and sailing courses start. The new boathouse (not open to visitors) is built on the site of the old slipway.

b. The entrance gate and courtyard
This narrow gate and steep steps is the only way of reaching the buildings on the Island and the higher levels where the upper battery was sited. The construction of this way was quite deliberate. The two gates, with their heavy doors (one is now missing) would make an attack on the Island through them almost impossible as this entrance would come directly under fire from the sentry walk close to the crane and the musket ledge in the small courtyard. Climb to this and one can see how the entrance way was well defended. The lifting tackle originally used over 100 years ago, positioned on a protruding granite ledge, is also still there. The yard is a sun trap and quite a few plants flourish here. The stonework dates from Tudor times.

Part of the early wall defences on the Island's western side.

c. The Commanding Officer's house — Island House
This is the first building on the left after passing through the narrow entrance. It is now being used by the staff of the Adventure Centre as living quarters and administrative offices in a manner similar to its former use. This was constructed between 1830 and 1835 as part of an extensive scheme of fortification and may well have replaced older buildings on this site.

d. Steps and ramp
These have been included in these notes as they were an aid in getting the heavy guns and equipment on to the higher levels. It must be remembered that the early guns were probably man-handled with the use of the lifting gear still in position by the entrance. The slope was used for hauling up materials, etc., and possibly the island's fire engine. A large ring is still fixed to the wall at the top of the slope through which ropes or chains could be worked.

e. Barrack block
This building was also constructed during the 1830's and its use has not changed. There has, of course, been a change of occupants and some internal modifications for its present use but its appearance remains almost unaltered from that decade. The officer's accommodation was at the west end where there are three storeys while the non-commissioned ranks occupied the rest of the building as living and sleeping quarters. A wall plaque commemorates the renovation of the building and its opening by the Rt. Hon. Viscount Amory in 1971.

f. The ablution block
The original name for this earlier building behind the barrack block has been included in these notes. The use of it has certainly not changed from the time it was constructed in 1790. The finely cut limestone blocks are more fitting to their setting on the island than the later buildings and are much to the credit of its builders.

g. The sentry walk
Now follow the lower path behind the commanding officer's house but do not go into the tunnel. Turn left and pass under the newly constructed crane (it replaces one that was built during the last war) and then carefully cross into the narrow walk from which sentries maintained guard behind its limestone wall and musket openings. It will be seen that this position gives a good view over the slipway and entrance gate area. This walk is of the same period as the entrance. Now return to the tunnel.

h. Entrance tunnel to casemates
This covered way, to use its original description, is part of a series of tunnels through which access could be gained to the casemates and their guns on the eastern side of the island. The various tunnels and accompanying shell and cartridge stores were well

protected from attack. Go through the tunnel and, to the right, will be seen the entrance to five store rooms constructed to hold supplies of ammunition. These are linked on their far side to the casemates by two tunnels cutting through the island along which the heavy shells were carried. Immediately behind the casemates were more underground rooms designated as *expense magazines*. Follow the tunnel until it reaches the beginning of the casemates.

The island buildings from the upper battery.

i. The casemates

This massive scheme of construction was undertaken during the 1860's as a direct result of the danger brought about by the French navy using, for the first time, steam-driven warships clad with iron with an increased fire power. This scheme cost in the region of £63,500 which included the upper battery works. The casemates were planned to hold 12 ton guns protected by very heavy iron shields. The manner in which they worked is not difficult to see and the command they gave over the main deep water channel into the docks will be readily appreciated. Access to one or two is still possible and a few wall fittings are still in position.

Now follow the inner walk around to the end of the casemates then back noting the entrances into the island on the left. The front of the casemates is accessible from the entrance at the end of the covered way while a very good view of the Sound can be had from the casemate roof. Access to this is up to the narrow spiral steps at the beginning of the casemates. This complex of stonework and tunnels is quite unique and amply demonstrates the extent to which our Victorian predecessors went to defending this country.

j. The upper battery

This occupies the highest ground on the island and is readily accessible up the short path from behind the barrack block. The fortifications here are mainly of two periods. The first dates from the extensive works undertaken during the 1860's as part of the plans including the casemates and the second the remains of gun emplacements and service tunnels constructed during World War I. Both building schemes obliterated much earlier work and these in turn took the place of the old St. Michael's chapel.

It is safe to assume that this higher ground has been built on many times with the consequence that the chances of finding or working out the positions of the very early fortifications are very small.

The most recent and, perhaps the most exciting, find was the extremely large guns set up in the 1860's known then as the *upper battery*. Since their discovery it has been found that they were cast in Newcastle-upon-Tyne between 1869-70 and put into service in 1871. Three 11 inch calibre guns and one of 12 inch calibre each of 25 tons were cast in iron and gave a muzzle velocity of 1,360 ft/second using a charge of 85 lbs. of black powder. On testing they could penetrate thirteen inch armour at a 1,000 yards. The smaller gun is a Georgian cast iron sea-service cannon of the period 1790-1820. The large guns were painted green and mounted en barbette with earthern traverses between them. (*Barbette:* an earthern terrace inside the parapet of a rampart serving as a platform for heavy guns.) What a sight these must have been but what a great loss that there are no photographs of them in position!

k. The oubliette prison

This is thought to be the oldest building on the Island. It was used for holding prisoners. Its size and shape suggests that men were dropped through an opening in its roof and left there to die. As yet there is no definite proof of this practice here although this did happen in medieval times in France. The building is in front of the near end of the casements.

l. Gun emplacements

These are the relatively modern gun positions running more or less east to west along the crown of the Island. They date from about the time of the Great War and were partly modernised to cope with attacks during the last war. There is the centre group of three flanked on either side by smaller guns linked to service passages for the supply of ammunition. These positions were partly destroyed when the army vacated the island in the early 1960's although the shell hoists are still in position and some of the metal work for supporting the guns.

m. Western musket wall

This substantial limestone wall is thought to have been constructed just prior to the Civil War in the 1640's and was obviously the island's main defence on this side. Muskets would have covered this flank and the nearby Little Drake's Island through the openings in the wall. One part of it appears to form the upper section of a room or store which runs down to the level of the rocks.

n. Little Drake's Island

This is the small island on the western side which can be reached via the steps erected in front of the barrack block. There is also a beach here which is very popular in the summer. A close view of the *Dragon's teeth*, the *Bridge* and remains of a wartime barge can be seen at low tide from the rocks to the south of this islet. To the left of this position is the rock face used by young people during their adventure courses. One interesting relic of the days of the sailing ships is a hauling ring fixed to the rocks facing Plymouth by means of which ships could be hauled against unfavourable winds.

A hauling ring for ships of the last century.

Part of the sentry walk overlooking the entrance gate.

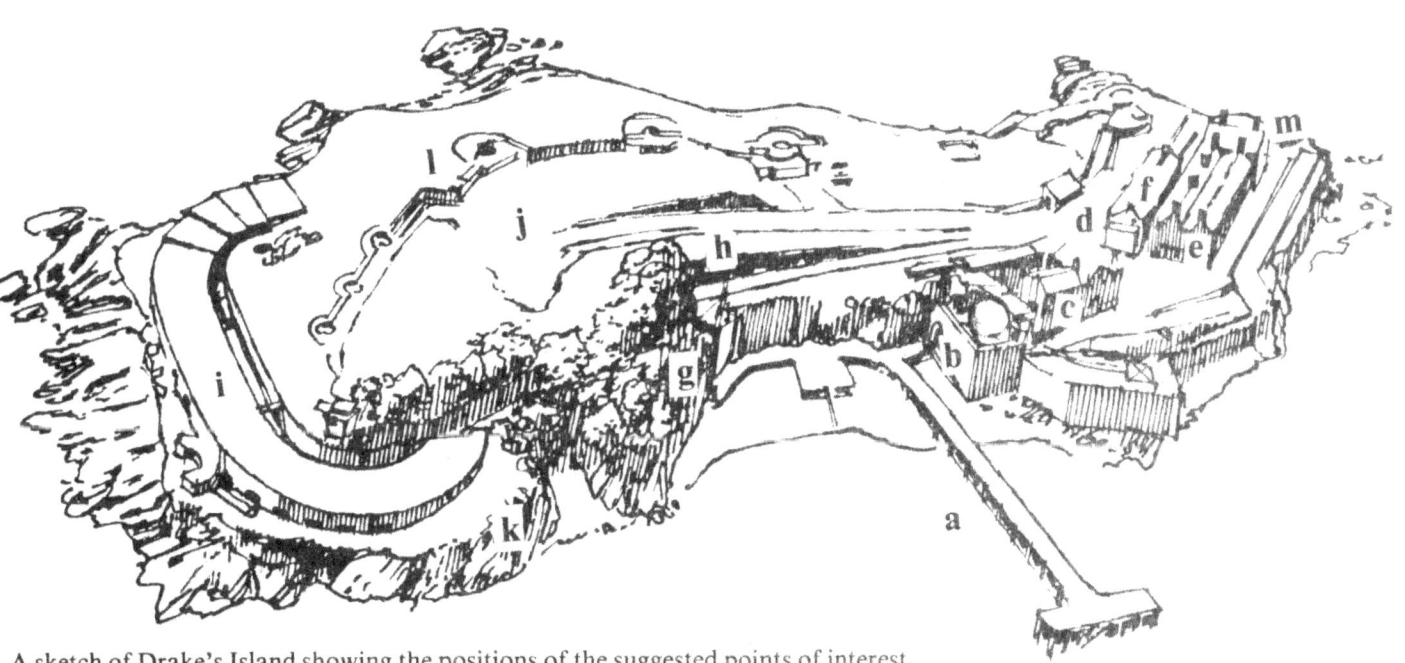
A sketch of Drake's Island showing the positions of the suggested points of interest.

The tunnel or covered way leading to the casemates.

The island's oubliette-styled building facing the north shore.

Two nineteenth century engravings of Plymouth Sound showing Drake's Island from the mainland.

Arthur L. Clamp – the man behind the books

Arthur Leslie Clamp was a man of boundless energy with a passion for helping others, particularly through his love of history. A printer by trade, he started his career in a printing company before moving his family from Exeter to Plymouth to teach at the Plymouth College of Art and Design, where he eventually became the Head of the Printing Department.

Arthur with his five children.

A Devoted Family Man

Despite his love of teaching, Arthur prioritised his family, always making it home by 5:30pm for tea. He and his wife, Rosemary, raised five children: Susan, Angela, Elizabeth, David, and Steven. Arthur would often combine his love of family and history by taking his children on Sunday walks, encouraging them to appreciate historical monuments by taking photos or making crayon rubbings of gravestones for his books. The family home at 203 Elburton Road was a hub of activity, with a large garden, featuring a two-storey fort and a makeshift swimming pool.

A Lifelong Learner and Adventurer

Arthur's thirst for knowledge extended beyond history to a deep curiosity about the world. He was passionate about exploring different cultures, traditions, and cuisines, often taking advantage of his long summer holidays as a teacher to travel to places like India, Russia, South America, the middle east and the USA, sometimes bringing one of his children along. This adventurous spirit even influenced his home life, as seen by the short-lived family tradition of steam-cooking vegetables after a trip to Iceland.

History is a prominent feature of family days out

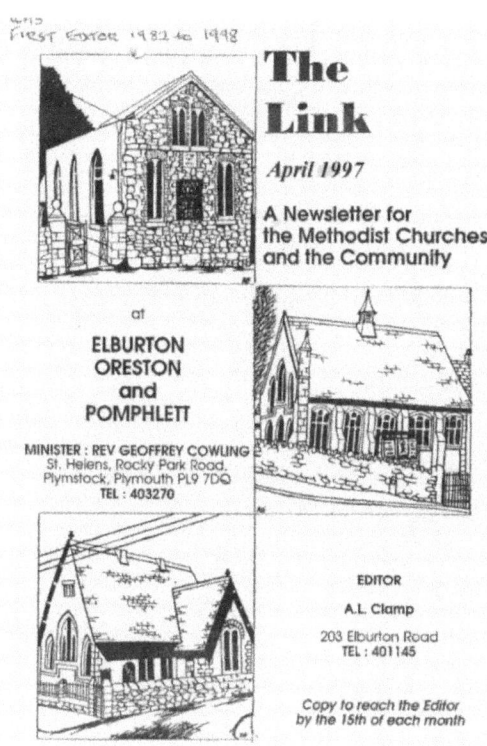

Community and Philanthropic Spirit

His commitment to serving others was evident in his long-standing involvement with the Elburton Methodist Church. He was the Sunday School Superintendent for over 15 years and served as the editor of the wider church's monthly newsletter, "The Link," for a similar duration. After Rosemary's very sad passing, Arthur later remarried and, following a chance encounter with a professor from India, established a connection with a missionary school in Chennai. Together with his new wife, Christine, he co-founded a "Sponsor a Child's Education" program that continues to this day.

Pictured left – The cover of 'The Link' complete with hand drawn sketches of each church by Angela
Below right – Arthur Clamp promoting his latest book
Below left – Arthur at home with his first wife, Rosemary
Below centre – Arthur on holiday with his second wife, Christine

A Legacy of Learning and Positivity

Arthur's greatest passion was history, which he brought to life through tireless research, documentation, and the many books he authored. He was driven by a need to "never be stuck in a rut," constantly seeking new experiences, meeting new people, and expanding his knowledge. With a positive attitude and a great sense of humour, he was always ready to help others, leaving a lasting impact on his family and community. His children, Susan, Angela, Elizabeth, David, and Steven, remember him with love and gratitude.

David Clamp, 2025

A Legacy of Local History

Below is the story of how Arthur L Clamp began writing books, in his own words, drafted shortly before he passed away in 2001. I have only made minor alterations to this text, correcting grammatical errors that he did not survive to correct himself. When I first discovered this text, I was shocked to see my name mentioned. It seems that, unbeknownst to me, I shared my first PC with him. I suspect he used it during the day when I was at school, although I do have one memory of sitting with him and showing him how it worked. It has been a pleasure to pick up where he left off and see his books republished and redistributed, and to know that I was part of the story, even back then. It was also fascinating to discover that his pricing structure matches the way I have tried to price the books, with a third going to local sellers and the rest covering printing costs with a little left over for my expenses.

I am his eldest grandson, and it is a privilege to curate his legacy, which we are calling 'The Clamp Collection'. The very last line of the text originally reads "The following pages list all the titles." Sadly, that page is missing and we have no record of all the books he published and knowing that some of those were researched by other authors makes the process of finding them even harder. I look forward to one day completing the collection and seeing them all available again. And maybe, one day, I'll even start writing my own to add to the series. For now, here is his story in his own words.

Steven Gibson, 2025

Writing and Publishing Booklets on Local Topics and Areas

I started this interest in either 1968 or 1969 when living in Woodford. I had by these dates established the Department of Printing and I think I must have been looking for something different to do. The first titles were of A5 size proofed from type set at Clarke, Doble and Brendon, Ltd., Plymouth printers, and then made up into pages and printed at Sawtell and Neilson, Ltd., Totnes.

Then began a slow process of getting them out to shops, etc. which proved to be more time consuming and difficult than actually researching, writing and getting the books into print. However, I persisted and opened a business account with Barclays Bank on the Broadway. I was advised to give it a title so I called it "Westway Publications". There came along another problem, one of storage of paper and finished books which was solved when the family moved to Elburton in 1970.

I changed the printer to Penwell, Ltd., Callington, Cornwall, as he was then just setting up himself and his prices seemed very reasonable. I did not get any of the printers to make up the complete books. I hand folded the flat printed sheets, stitched the books on a small manual table stitcher and trimmed them in a small hand turned guillotine which I bought from someone in Penzance for £40. It was brought up in a van.

The trouble and time going to and fro to Callington was too much so I transferred the printing to PDS Printers, Prince Rock, Plymouth, and I have been with them ever since. Now they are at Plympton which is easy to reach and they fold the flat sheets which was turning out to be a long chore which only saved a small part of the printing costs.

All my first titles were written by myself. I took the photographs and developed them in the loft of the house, the type was set by now on a computer situated in the house at Elburton from which I had collected photographic lengths of text to cut up and law down as pages.

At some point I decided that I would do my own film processing of lith film so I bought a large second hand process camera from Kingsbridge and learnt through trial and error to make line negatives of the text and halftone negatives of the illustrations which proved more difficult than I anticipated. The main problem was trying to keep the developer in the large dish at the correct temperature as any change would affect the developing time. I replaced this old camera with a brand new one bought from Croydon, Surrey, costing £900. This has turned out to be a great asset cutting out an expensive part of the printer's costs and one crucial aspect of the work which I could control.

By the middle 1970s there were many outlets I had contacted in Plymouth, up to Dartmoor, Exeter, around to Torbay, Totnes, Dartmouth and the South Hams. The market for local books was much greater than I had first thought and through getting to know many local people undertaking research themselves had the chance to help and make up books for other people who had in most instances, got together a collection of photographs with some text in a rather muddled way. Through my experience in print I was able to shape up their work and get it into print and in every case I had to pay the printer and let the person have the royalties. In the majority of titles produced in this manner this was another way of producing titles and it did give some profit to my work. However, I must say that in a few cases I lost out by either the other person getting the numbers wrong, not returning any monies from stock I delivered or they thought that more of their books should have been sold.

The print run was usually 1,000 copies and from time to time I have had reprints of 250 copies. It took about ten years to clear the first print run so I always had large stocks in the garage, workshop, etc. The numbers sold during the early years was about 7,000 copies a year increasing to around 9,000 copies and for the whole of the enterprise about 500,000 have been sold. The booklets have become part of the local scene and many people collect them, shops regularly order copies and I go around certain areas month by month restocking or replacing titles as necessary.

During the past year or so I have started setting the text on a Packard Bell PC, something which I should have done some years back. I share it with Steven Gibson, my grandson. There appears to be no end to the market for local books, but I could not earn a regular income because of the long time it takes to sell stock.

However, now exceeding 100 titles made up mainly of A4 twenty-four page booklets, some folded guides, with selling prices set with a third going to the shop which is the trade custom, the original idea has been quite successful and could go on for ever.

Apart from monetary benefits, however spasmodically these might be, I have learnt a lot myself, met many interesting people and have become part of the local scene with requests to give talks and to advise people about getting into print.

Arthur L Clamp, 2001

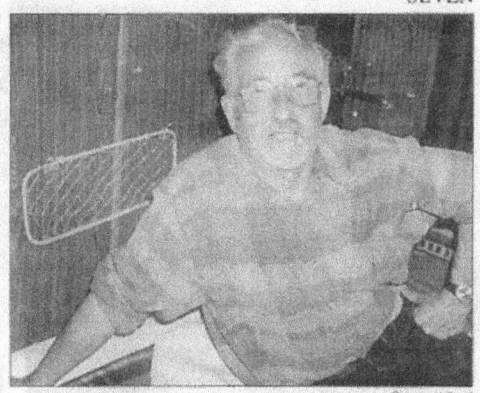

This newspaper article, published by the Evening Herald on 17th August 2001, forms a good record of his life. Just as he encourages us to learn more about local history, we encourage you to learn a little about him. For that reason, we have included these pages at the back of all the most recently republished books, in honour of his memory and recognition of his contribution to the community.

www.ingramcontent.com/pod-product-compliance
Lightning Source LLC
Chambersburg PA
CBHW061409070526
44584CB00031B/4196